MY SECRET MOTHER

"an adoptee speaks to the girls who went away"

ROBERT J. BANNON

READERS COMMENTS

"...My Secret Mother is a good read."

Joan Vanstone

Parent Finders

"...this is a very powerful book...
...a very personal and moving look at the issue of
adoption..."

Yvonne Jeffrey

Calgary Herald

"I just wanted to say how very much I enjoyed
reading your heartfelt book... you have an excellent
way of wording your ideas."

JFS

London, Ontario

"...fearless and courageous...you stirred my own
reflections."

HC

Calgary, Alberta

"Bob Bannon has written a love letter that creates the bridge between mother and child that every adopted person and the mothers who gave birth to them, longs for. Sensitive, articulate and real, My Secret Mother reveals the unspoken conversation that the adopted child has with themselves. Bob's clever use of the reflected question opens the dialogue between child and mother while understanding and yes, even gratitude rushes in. This book is recommended reading to all of my clients dealing with adoption issues. It will, I believe, be in the lending library of counselors and coaches everywhere who are working with birth mothers (and fathers) and adoptees."

Kerry Parsons

Director

Center for Inspired Living

MY SECRET MOTHER

"an adoptee speaks to the girls who went away"

by Robert J. Bannon

e ISBN 9781470148041

original editing by Yvonne Jeffrey

other books by Robert J. Bannon

THE WEST COAST TRAIL: One Step at a Time

ISBN   9780973964608

e ISBN 97809739646-2-2

THE ONE HOUR AUTHOR

non-fiction book writing for busy people

e ISBN 97809739646-3-9

Dedicated, with love, to every young woman who had to "go away"

Friday, July 27, 2007 - 9:30 AM

"Hello."

"Mr. Bannon?"

"Yes it is. May I help you?"

"Is this Mr. Robert Bannon?"

"Yes. Who is this?"

"Mr. Bannon, this is _____ from the Province of Ontario, Social Services Department. About 5 years ago, you sent in a request to our department inquiring about your birth father. Is that correct?"

"Yes, I did do that."

"Mr. Bannon, I just got off the phone after speaking with your father."

"……..

"……..

"Mr. Bannon, are you still there?"

Standing in the middle of a warehouse speaking to two co-workers, the noise from the fork lift and the music blaring over the loudspeakers began growing in volume. I couldn't hear and my knees were getting wobbly. A strange queasiness rumbled in my stomach as I walked through the spots dancing in my eyes, toward the exit door, in order to escape from the noise. I needed to concentrate on this unbelievable information being emitted from my cell phone.

"I… I don't know what to say. I didn't think that he would even be alive."

"Yes, he is fairly old but he is very much alive. You had requested health information about him and he has given me his medical history. Would you like me to fax it to you?"

"Ah, yes that would be great."

"He is hard of hearing and quite old now but I can tell you that he is in excellent health. He was quite shocked to learn that he had a son."

"I didn't expect him to be alive."

"Because of his age and his hearing, he does not want to meet with you but he wishes you well and good luck in the rest of your life."

"This is amazing. Can I tell you something that happened earlier today?"

"Of course."

"I'm a writer and I wrote a book about my adoption. I finished many months ago and it has been sitting on my desk since then. Just a couple of hours ago, I contacted my editor to see if she would like to take on the project of helping me with it because I had finally decided, last night, to release it. I wonder if he would have any interest in reading it?"

"Mr. Bannon, you may be aware that this department is closing down at the end of next month and we are not sure what procedures will be in place for searching for adoption information. Once we have made connection with a birth parent and they have refused further contact, we are not supposed to release any further details or contact them again. But, because of this information, I am going to make an exception in this case and I will get back to you with his reply."

I sat at my desk, having returned to my office, and felt a little numb as I tried to put a lifetime of confusion and fear of this moment into some kind of order. My breathing had just returned to normal when my cell phone began its familiar vibrating on my hip.

"Bob, here."

"Mr. Bannon, I just got off the phone with your father and he would very much like to read your book."

My Secret Mother

"In all of us there is a hunger, marrow-deep, to know our heritage, to know who we are – and where we have come from. Without this enriching knowledge, there is a hollow yearning, there is the most disquieting – loneliness."
Arthur Haley, author "ROOTS"

COMMUNION

I reclined on a remote beach on the west coast of Vancouver Island, my body cocooned by the coarse, still warm sand, resting my head on a smooth ocean washed log. With my eyes softly closed, I could feel myself surrounded by the cool black night air as I listened to the rhythmic heartbeat of the Pacific waves pound the shoreline. No seagulls, traffic or human voices to pierce the communion of nature as I stood solitary witness to the harmony of land and sea. My eyelids slowly rolled up allowing me to view the countless crystals of light as they glowed and winked against the backdrop of endless ink blue sky. The heavens continued to unfold the canopy of bright white stars but curiously, none of the light penetrated to this corner of the universe, save the glow of the moon as it reflected off the black rolling water.

My eyes adjusted to the scene before me and I began to observe and feel myself drawn into the infinite abyss of the night sky, full of mystery and longing. Answers lay out there just beyond the questions still unformed in my mind. Objects chased through the stars, evidenced by their tails of light, they randomly appeared and then disappeared just as quickly – elusive, unpredictable and unattainable as they danced beyond my grasp. I was a stranger there as I watched, an observer, unable to become part of the symphony of life but merely there to record the spectacle as it played out on the stage in front of me. In time, I allowed my eyelids to bring down the curtain on this scene and return to the meditative half-state between reality and promise. I drew breath deeply into my diaphragm and felt the moment expanding in my core. I felt a flutter in the pit of my belly as I balanced between air and ground, a diaphanous spirit hovering above my physical being to, once again, act the observer in my own life. Not quite belonging to either world, attached to neither solid ground nor cool night air, I felt separate and alone while still tethered to the idea of humanity. Feeling the link to my own source at a depth previously unassailed, I was lured by the call of the sea as it drew me home. The ache in my heart, once just a whisper on the ocean breeze, grew stronger as I grasped for solid Terra Firma. It was the perfect metaphor for my life as the search for the meaning of my existence had begun to take place. I might presume that the clues will be elusive and I should probably begin with the question of who my mother and father are. The question had been tantalizing me for decades and for some reason unknown, it was finally time to unlock a door that had been shut by my own indifference.

ME

I began writing this book the day I was told that I had been adopted. I don't remember if it was the telling that caused me to feel different or if it was the telling that explained why I had always felt so different. I was quite young, but old enough to understand that my parents were no longer my mother and father. In some way, I lost all four that afternoon as I sat on the edge of my bed and listened to the woman I used to think was my mother tell me about adoption. If I was given any other information at the time, I suspect I was too blindsided to hear it. The subject was never revisited by my parents. I was expected to put this tidal wave that had turned my world upside down, behind me. Apparently, I didn't need to know any more since it was all now shrouded in secrecy. Without any input from me, I had gone from being a son to being a secret! I proceeded to govern myself accordingly for almost five decades.

Until my early fifties, I managed to stumble through life without doing too much internal exploration. I steadfastly maintained an ambivalent attitude toward my adoption, carefully refusing to investigate the matter and thus neatly avoiding the need to explore any of my inner confusion and turmoil. Several decades of frustration and undirected anger simmered below the surface, showing itself occasionally, as I fought the idea of becoming a victim, yet feeling that I had never reached any of the potential that I knew I possessed. Potential was a word that I came to hate. From my earliest memories of school, teachers constantly told me that I had so much "potential." Employers, who cared to notice, continued the theme into my working life. I knew it myself but I had no idea how to break out of the cart path I was following and begin to utilize and fulfill some of this "potential." It became a downward spiral as I tried and failed, got up, tried again, failed again, new job, different city, self-employment, lots of potential, no finish, failed again, frustration, anger, everyone else's fault but I knew where the responsibility came to rest. It was with me! What the hell was wrong with me?

The magic elixir was handed over the prescription counter at the drugstore in a little plastic bottle containing something called anti-depressants. The world's largest selling group of drugs would now smooth out my mood swings, make me more palatable to my loved ones and generally create a catatonic lifestyle that left me mood-less and direction-less but ever so pleasant. The frustration and anger still bubbled away but I just couldn't feel it anymore. The symptom was cured but the cause remained undiagnosed and out of reach.

I began to reclaim my life when I was invited to participate in the Odyssey Journey by the program's creators and my friends of many years. Odyssey became a journey of the spirit that helped me look below the surface of my day-to-day existence to discover the truth that I could never quite reach. Mostly, it was a truth that I had denied. Two more journeys quickly followed as I decided to hike the West Coast Trail, one of the planet's outstanding backpacking experiences. No backwoods camper was

I, but the planning, preparation and completion of this seven day journey was a tale I shared with family and close friends upon my return. It was the experience of a lifetime. They encouraged me to write down some of the stories, which I began to do. This resulted in my next journey: the writing and publishing of my first book, "The West Coast Trail: One Step at a Time." Prescription drugs dropped long ago in the training for the Trail, my life was now available for the next journey when happenstance produced a book called "The Girls Who Went Away."

Ms. Fessler's book created another major turn in the highway of my life as it opened a whole new world to me. The world of unwed mothers. I had one of those! In the interviews published in the book, I was shocked to learn that most girls who had given up their children also lived with the same feelings of abandonment, loss, anger and pain that I endured. I had never considered life from my own mother's point of view until then. It turned everything I thought

I knew about my adoption story, on its head. I felt a strong need to respond in some way.

How could I go through life without acknowledging that my own birth mother probably joined the hundreds of thousands of other women who lived in a state of guilt and shame, left to fend for themselves, as the memory of a baby given away, haunted them to their grave? It was probably too late to tell my own mother, she would be well into her eighties, but I was determined to let other birth mothers know how so many of us long-remembered children, umbilical cords still attached, have a longing to remove the guilt, shame, blame and anger from the table. We've all spent too long locked up in emotions buried unexpressed, loyalties misdirected, lives left unlived, waiting and wondering. Wondering about the who's, the where's and the why's. The answers buried in filing cabinets that have been locked by bureaucracy and indifference.

This is a letter of love written to my own birth mother but meant to include all of those courageous young women who endured society's glares of judgment. Despite options available to them, they allowed life a chance in the belief that giving up their baby would result in their child having a better life. Many have lived in silence, still carrying a heavy burden thrust upon them by the very people they trusted the most.

I am here to tell you that you are thought about every day, your courage recognized and your loneliness shared. Grateful for your sacrifice, think of me as the voice unheard, speaking with great respect and even love, the unvarnished truth, to the girls who went away.

WONDER

Here's the thing Mom, I don't now, nor did I ever, blame you for putting me up for adoption. I spent most of my life being very careful to avoid using adoption to explain any of my inner feelings, conflicts, loneliness, confusion, anger, depression and a general overriding sense of simply not belonging. What I know is that I would not exist if you hadn't become pregnant. I wouldn't exist had you not decided to carry me to birth. I would not be who I am, had you not "given me up."

I don't know if you gave me up willingly or were forced to by the prevailing attitudes of a post war society that deemed unwed mothers unfit. You have never been "unfit" to me. How could I ever think of the woman who gave me life as unfit? I don't judge you for anything you have done because I know that without you, there is no me. I feel gratitude for that. I also feel great empathy and sympathy for the pain that my creation may have brought to you.

I've been looking at this whole adoption issue from only my own point of view for my entire life. It has recently come to my attention that there is another paradigm – yours. It has also come to my attention that perhaps you have spent your entire life wondering about me. Having read a few things about "birth mothers," I find it absolutely amazing how similar some of our issues are. Issues that show up like our feelings of abandonment, loneliness, emptiness, difference along with the idea of not knowing, holding a secret, longing, afraid to interfere, not being good enough and all those emotionally charged fears and challenges that have haunted both of us. Frankly, I can't believe that I have never considered adoption from your perspective before. How difficult it must have been to allow the baby that you carried for nine months, to be taken away from you. The pangs of guilt, the remorse and the second guessing must have been a constant reminder. Were you told that your baby would have a better life if someone else raised him? A better life without you? Were you told that a doctor or business man or some economically stable, perhaps even wealthy father and a wonderful, intelligent, stay at home mom would raise your child to the success and accomplishment you could never hope to do? From what I have read, those were common stories told to expectant young girls who were encouraged to put this whole episode "behind them." Were you able to put me behind you or have you, like me, spent the rest of your life wondering?

I am not going to apply the moralities, standards and political correctness of today to a decision that you were probably forced into making as a young woman. Many years ago unmarried, pregnant women were ostracized, denounced, hidden and shamed. Today's society seems to celebrate the pregnant, unmarried, single, mom-to-be. It was not the case in your day! I understand that. If you need me to forgive you for that, then I truly do forgive you, but I also understand

and I am absolutely grateful to you. If you had not had the courage to carry me to term, to suffer the slings and arrows of a buttoned up, narrow minded, unforgiving society, then I would not exist today – thank you! I hope that some of your courage has passed down to me.

You may be wondering what I've been doing, thinking and feeling since you gave birth to me and how adoption has influenced my life. Most people may not think of this but I have no way of relating to life as a "natural" born child of my parents, sometimes referred to as normal children (so what does that make me)? Consequently, I can't compare my life as an adoptee to the so called normal life as a child of birth parents. As far as I am concerned, my life was "normal" to me, at least until I got older and began to see some differences through a historical perspective. I feel lucky because I was adopted by a couple who were good, honest, hard working, caring and rarely ever made me feel unwanted. I suspect that they were viewed somewhat skeptically by their own families when they adopted two children, starting with me a couple of years after they married. They never shared their reasons with me but I tuned into some unexpressed ripples at quite an early age. There may have been another reason for feeling different in my adoptive mother's case as she was born with a hearing deficit. This is something I will return to later.

Both of my adoptive parents were very religious. Roman Catholicism played a major role in my young life as we went to mass every Sunday, more often at Easter and Christmas and I spent most of my school years being taught by priests and nuns, acting as an altar boy for many years, studying the catechism and going to countless family funerals and weddings. Everything revolved around the church. Both of my adoptive parents came from big Irish Catholic families full of kids, nuns, tears, fights, song, whiskey, roast beef and mashed potatoes, heart break, laughter, dark suspicions, sweepstakes tickets, tragedy, large family gatherings and small mixed farms. As a young child, I don't think I was aware of my being different or not belonging but as I approached and entered my teens that awareness began to seep in around the edges of my consciousness.

Some of that feeling can be attributed to the usual teen angst but I seem to have been endowed with a fairly strong dose of intuition. Did this come from you? I've always had the ability to feel some of the deeper dimensions of people around me. I've been able to hear deep seated requests or truth expressed by family members, customers, fellow employees and so on, when others didn't appear to be able to. Of course, it's hard to know if this gift is hereditary or environmental. I have given credit for my ability to hear the real words of others to my adoptive mother. She was hard of hearing throughout her life. When I was young, this presented an enormous source of frustration and sometimes embarrassment for me. Neither of us knew at the time that she was teaching me to listen and speak. In order to be heard by someone who is hard of hearing, the speaker must enunciate very clearly and project those words so that the listener can understand. Those skills came in handy as I spent much of my high school life in several stage acting roles – something that I wish I had pursued into adulthood, as I could slip into a clearly defined persona, a place I have yet to find for myself.

In recent years I have given much thought to my mother's hearing problem and realize that it was one of the things that set her apart in her family. With some reason, she always felt that people were talking about her, mimicking and making fun, even as she stood in the same room. I saw evidence of that within the extended family and frankly, I know it happened in our home as well. What loneliness, abandonment and a feeling of being ostracized she must have experienced. Years after her death, when I finally came to this realization, I began to understand that we shared much in common. Now, I realize that you, my birth mother, may have felt the similar pain of loneliness and separation and so it feels like a completed circle as this unexpected connection forms and expands. My adoptive parent, my birth mother and I, alone, and unknowingly connected in a way that is unique and amazing. These are the kinds of things that have occurred to me throughout my life as I pursue the truth of my real self. I wonder if you have ever explored this side of yourself and I wonder if this quest that my life feels like, is in some measure, a result of being your son? Obviously it is! Once again, I have a reason to express my gratitude to you for creating me.

I often wonder what you did after my birth. Did you return to your family, your work and your life and what was that like? Were you welcomed back, were you forgiven or did you need to be forgiven? Most importantly, were you loved and accepted? I wonder why you didn't marry my father. I was told, in the Children's Aid Society information letter, that he wanted to marry you. Is that true? I am somewhat skeptical (a natural state of being for me) of that information – are you a skeptic too?

Naturally, I am very curious about the rest of your life. I'm curious about whether or not you married, whether or not you had other children. That is one of the reasons that has prevented me from searching very hard for you and now I fear that it is too late. One of the scenarios that has always gone through my mind is that you may have a family that doesn't know about me. The last thing I would ever want to do is put you in a position that would hurt you. That has always been a fear that combines with the common adoption affliction of not being wanted or of being rejected again. It continues to be incredibly powerful and limiting.

Perhaps I inherited some of my attitudes from you. I am always very conscious of the hurt inflicted upon others and have spent my life not wanting to be the source of that hurt. I wish I could say that I was successful in that wish as I know that I have hurt other people. Perhaps the best way I can describe this is that I am always acutely aware of the hurt that other people experience. Tears well up frequently when I witness "hurt" – tears that I have been successful at hiding. Further to the point though, the pain I experience when I witness other people being hurt has moved into a sense of wanting to please others. That is a position I have held all of my life. While not always possible, I most often position myself to please others which would explain a life spent in some sort of sales arena. Like so much of my life, I have no idea if this trait is in any way connected to adoption. It is part of who I am regardless of its source but it does present another form of confusion since, in my heart, I have never found a sense of satisfaction from my career.

I can't tell you why I haven't made a bigger effort to learn more about you prior to this. Part of the reason is explained by my not wanting to bring more hurt or shame to you but there is more to it. When my own son was about to be born, we felt that we needed some medical history from me, something I never had. I discussed this with my sister who was also adopted and she provided me with a contact at the Children's Aid Society in the town where the adoption order was finalized. A letter to this same social worker resulted in a much appreciated four page reply full of non-identifying information.

When I look back at this, it is almost unbelievable to me, but I put that letter in a file folder marked "Bob's adoption" and totally forgot about its existence for the next sixteen or seventeen years! It was as though I had blocked it from my mind. The file folder sat in our filing cabinet, moved from city to city and home to home with us until one day many years later I sucked up the courage to look for you. It had remained unknown, or at least unacknowledged for those many years. In my early fifties by this time, I was doing some exploration into myself with the help of a friend who is coincidentally, also adopted. I had listened to her for many years talk about her adoption and the incredible influence that it had on her life. I was unable to understand her obsession because I didn't see that adoption meant much to me at all. I refused to consciously blame adoption for any ills that befell me, for any doubts about who I was – I simply ignored the whole issue, much like I ignored, "put out of my mind"- the letter from the social worker.

As a sop to my friend, I agreed to initiate a search for my birth parents and contacted the government department responsible for adoption information in the province of my birth. I did this in great fear that you were waiting for me to do so and a reunion might be expected and I wasn't sure I was ready for that. I mailed my letter and waited with great trepidation for a phone call requesting some sort of meeting. Instead I received an envelope full of brochures and forms to fill out. In order to fill in the blanks and boxes required, I needed to find my long ignored manila file folder marked "Bob's adoption" and there was the letter along with original court documentation and records received by me many years prior. I found the information requested and filled out the documentation and at some point sent it back to the provincial government and then held my breath in a mixture of fear, anxiety and hope. There was a familiarity in this combination of feelings. These were feelings that I had harbored deeply, quietly and silently for a long time.

While I had never wanted to blame adoption for my failings, I had looked to the fact of adoption to rescue me from those same failings. When I look back on it, I'm not very proud of the person I had created. There seems to have been a very long stretch of years when all I thought about was drinking, partying and carousing. I did all three to excess. I ignored everything else including education, employment, relationships and money. Well I didn't exactly ignore money – I was highly conscious of its existence. Whenever it existed in my pocket, I could pursue drinking which meant I could do some partying and with a little luck, some carousing would unfold. Not very often, and certainly not on any consistent basis, did the paying of bills or upholding of other responsibilities ever take any precedence. I was constantly lurching from one set of problems to another and I always thought that more money was the solution. I didn't pay my bills until they were in the hands of some nasty collection agency. I never really made any headway in my jobs – too many late, drunk nights to be motivated during the day. I always seemed to be involved in a significant relationship and somehow managed to attract some incredible women to me. In sober, aging retrospect I have always been unable to understand why any of the ladies I went out with, created short and long term relationships with, married (twice), ever gave me a second look, let alone a second chance. In some instances and especially in the case of my wife of over 30 years, third, fourth, fifth, 100th chances! Didn't they know who I was? My eye was constantly roving. I refused to accept responsibility, refused to commit myself, refused to talk about anything that mattered. Throughout those many years, I avoided as much of my life as possible and truly thought that my life's purpose revolved around my ability to pay for the next round of drinks. Courage was something found at the bottom of a scotch bottle. From that place came the ability to ask a beautiful woman to dance, to dream about career success and make promises I wouldn't keep the morning after.

I often tell the story about how I know that alcoholism is a real disease. I tried my best during those years to become a full fledged, card carrying member of the alcoholics club, without success. If sheer volume of consumption were enough to create an alcoholic, I would have been one by my twenty-first birthday. Apparently alcohol itself needs to connect up with some sort of physical element that I don't possess. One of the interesting things about my life is that most (not all) of the long term male friends that I've had have been recovering alcoholics and most of the women in my life have been very light drinkers. To this day, my long-suffering wife will look at me with a raised eye brow if I pour a third glass of wine, yet to me, my consumption has dropped to about 10% of what I used to drink. The third glass is usually left unfinished.

I've discovered that I used to drink to lose control. Being drunk allowed me to do, or at least try, things that I couldn't when sober. If I wasn't in control of myself, how could I be held responsible for my actions? This is kind of weird, to say the least, in someone who values a sense of control as highly as I do. These are some of the dichotomies that exist in my universe. Here's another one. Blaming adoption for my behavior was not something I was comfortable with. On the other hand, I had this underlying program operating in my head that felt like someone was watching me, perhaps even watching over me. I imagined, for whatever reason, that it was my birth father! Somehow, I had created this scenario that he was some sort of wealthy recluse and that when things got bad enough – he would rescue me from my debts, my boring employment and everything else I had created about my chaotic life.

I lived with that scenario for a large part of my life. I kept waiting to be rescued! I remember during the many stressful occasions that I created because I had partied the rent money away, gambled a pay check into small change and made unkeepable promises to the debt collectors, that one of the solutions that would miraculously appear to me was a lawyer with news of how my birth father was leaving me some vast fortune. One of the amazing experiences that I had in the research for this work was reading the account of an adopted man who used almost the identical language of his wait to be rescued, including the reclusive father, lawyer and inheritance. I now wonder if this is a common trait of adoptees.

It occurs to me that this fantasy I created may be partially responsible for my not searching for either of my birth parents. What if either one or both of you needed my help? I was in no position to help anybody so I hid from not only my birth parents, but everyone else as well.

I lived in a vicious circle of debt and drink, afraid of the phone ringing but desperate for someone to phone and save me. I was not a pretty picture during those years and adoption played such an interesting role as I balanced the absolute refusal to even think that it was in any way responsible for my various predicaments with the hope that this unknown benefactor would ride up on his white charger to my salvation.

Throughout that long winter of my discontent, to borrow a phrase, I steadfastly refused, as I do to this day, to place blame or responsibility for my misbehavior on you, mother. I have this feeling that to paint myself as a victim of adoption is an abdication of the responsibility I have for my own life. I know at my core level that you, my mother, the person who gave me life, are not to blame for what I chose to do with that life. There is lots of regret, guilt and anger to go around in this world and all of us would make significant changes in our decision making if given a second chance but please know this: I am eternally grateful for my life, my experience, my health and intelligence, my creativity and intuition, much of this inherited from you.

Without the circumstances that you put in motion, the being that I am, would not exist.

YOU

I wonder how you felt when you learned that you were pregnant with me? I wonder who told you. Your doctor? You probably suspected much earlier. Perhaps you even knew long before the confirmation was received. How were you informed? Was it in a supportive way or more likely, in a judgmental tone that was designed to make sure you felt guilty and ashamed? Did you carry that guilt with you along with me? Who was with you when you learned of your pregnancy? How did you feel deep down in that private place where no one else is allowed?

Based on the information supplied by the Children's Aid Society and the research that I've done into the prevailing attitudes of post World War II society in North America, I can't imagine a more repressive atmosphere than the one you must have encountered at that time in your life. I can only surmise the shame you must have been forced to feel. I always find it interesting that a couple of centuries ago, your ancestors and mine, fled continental Europe to escape the oppressive, religion based regimes that ruled the day. Boat loads arrived on the Eastern shores of North America in search of tolerance and freedom and then proceeded to duplicate the same kinds of prejudice and judgmental-ism that they sought refuge from. In post war Quebec, belonging to a large Roman Catholic family and discovering that you were about to become an unwed mother must have brought a special kind of terror.

According to the accounts I've read of other young women who found themselves in similar circumstance, you would have been accused of bringing unforgivable shame on your family. You may have been ostracized by your brothers and sisters – some more than others. Have you ever been able to reconcile with them? Do some still harbor judgment to this day? Were you made to feel unclean, unworthy, a "bad girl," damaged goods and all the horrible and degrading descriptions visited upon your peers of the time? For whatever comfort it can provide and from my own unique and maybe singular point of view, none of that opinion matters a wit to me! Sure, I have a very prejudicial perspective but now, these many years later, I hope that you will give value to that same perspective because regardless of whether or not we have met physically – we have been physically joined for nine months and emotionally joined for over sixty years. You have brought no shame to me. You have brought only life! What could be more valuable than that? Nothing could mean more to me than life itself. You are largely responsible for providing that life. Thank you!

It must have been confusing for young women in post war America to have glimpsed a new world as a result of being needed to step into the work force during the war. You and thousands more were encouraged to become partners in the war effort. Working in the factories and offices, you were made to feel that you were vital to the efforts of keeping the entire world free. You were given responsibility and a sense of empowerment for the first time in modern history. This was much more than the theoretical power of voting for the man who would represent your government interests. Instead, this power was on the ground, something you could hold in your hands with your pay packet. You had responsibility, freedom and economic clout.

What a confusing time it must have been as the servicemen returned from the European and far Eastern theatres of war and society assumed it would return to the old ways of running itself. I'm sure that the generation preceding yours, the generation in charge of the factories, schools, government, church and families naturally assumed that the women who had been expected to pitch in and keep industry running along with the home fires, would now simply step aside as their male counterparts returned to their rightful place at the head of the line. Is that what you were expected to do and did you? Why do I have this feeling that you resisted that subservient role? Why do I feel that I inherited this independent streak from you? Why do I suspect that you had discovered the world and decided to embrace it, step into it and become a full member of it rather than let it swallow you up and return you to some secondary role? Is that wishful thinking on my part? Have I simply idealized you as this strong, independent woman who refused to be bent into the shape that acceptable society demands? Did you use your intelligence to create a new and free world for yourself? The reason I wonder these things is that there is a common saying that implies that men seek to marry women that are like their mothers. The significant relationships throughout my life have all been with women who exhibit these same strong characteristics. I was never able to sustain a relationship with a woman who didn't value her own life first, acknowledge her abilities and strengths and live from a place of power. That presents its own set of challenges when two people value their own independence of action and thought as they bob and weave their way through the relationships of life, but I wouldn't have it any other way. The more I examine these characteristics in

47

myself, the more I come to believe that they had to be part of my make up at birth and that I am grateful to you for providing them to me. I can't imagine living life on any other terms.

When I ponder not only the circumstances but the prevailing attitudes, prejudices, assumptions and opinions that dominated society at the time of my birth, I am in awe of the courage that a young 22 year old woman displayed in deciding to carry me to term. Is it true that my father wanted to marry you? Is it true that he supported you financially through your pregnancy? Did you ever hear from him again? There are so many questions I have, so many things I would like to know about. Did you go on with your life, marry, have other children? Did you go through life with regret? Regret for having me, regret for "giving me up" or were you able to erase the memory like so many social workers, priests and parents of the day promised young women they would? My questions exist in two, perhaps three categories; questions about me, about you and about my father. I have spent my life denying the need for these answers. In truth, I have denied the need for formulating the questions. As I find myself in the autumn of my own life, I wonder and fear if I have waited too long to ask, too long to expect an answer. Another set of regrets to process! I've been afraid to ask the questions, perhaps now I am more afraid to find the answers. In the meantime, I am left to create fantasies about what was, what might have been, what is true and what is false. How about you, have you created fantasies, wondered about their validity, wondered about me?

Why do I get this overwhelming feeling that we both have spent our lives dancing around the outside of this issue because we are afraid to bring pain to the other? We live in our own pain, thinking we are sparing the other when, in fact the solution was to seek a reunion and dissolve the pain for both of us.

MY BIRTHDAY - SEPTEMBER 13

According to my birth certificate, I was born 63 years ago on this day. I have learned recently that many of these documents were falsified by the adoption agencies to maintain the heavy veil of secrecy. Be that as it may, at some point in time and in the vicinity of this date, you gave birth to me. I have only ever considered my birthday from my point of view: my age, whether it would allow me to vote, drink, or a milestone such as becoming 40 or 50. Now, with very mixed emotions, I am wondering how soon I'll be eligible for senior's discounts at the golf course. This year and this day, my feelings and thoughts go out to you instead. Does this day have significance for you? Do you celebrate it, loathe it or acknowledge it in any way?

I have usually tried to downplay my birth date. It seems to me a mixture of embarrassment and shyness. My wife insists on ensuring that it is acknowledged, otherwise I would prefer to let it slip by unnoticed.

According to the information currently available to me, you would, or already have, turned 85 this year, a milestone for sure. I recently helped my wife pick out an 80th birthday card for her own mother. I wonder what it would be like to give you one. Most importantly, how would you feel about receiving a birthday card from me? What would I write in it? What sort of greeting card company sentiment would be appropriate? How about something like, "To the Mother who gave me life itself."

I wonder if you mark this day or deny it. I wonder if your thoughts surrounding this date have changed over the years. I wonder, of course, if you are alive, well, happy, content, safe and sound of body, mind and spirit. These would be my birthday wish for you.

ROOTS

When I was growing up, the only other adopted kid that I was aware of, was my younger sister. I'm still a little jealous that her birth sister went to the effort of finding her after many years. My adopted sister was afraid to share much information with me, or the rest of the family, for fear of hurting us. I think she feared experiencing yet another abandonment. I'm not aware of any relationship developing between her and her older birth sister but at least a lot of questions were answered and my sister could put a face to her birth family. It allowed her to have a history.

I find myself in limbo when it comes to history and roots. I had an uncle, on my adoptive father's side who researched and wrote a family history, tracing it back to Ireland. This was interesting, if not my own. My adoptive mother's family traces its lineage back to Ireland and also Germany. I have very little detail beyond that. In neither case does it have anything to do with me so I live in some ways without a past other than the sketchy information provided by Family Services. As I think about it, even if I had the information about your family and my father's family, I don't suppose that history would feel much like mine either.

Whenever I am asked for a medical history, I reply that I was adopted and of course, the questioning stops immediately as if the questioner were embarrassed for prying too deeply into something even more personal than mere medical information. I haven't found that overly difficult because I have been blessed with good health. On the other hand, I also don't have any preconceived notions about what health issues I might face. Consequently, I have no predisposition to any medical ailments, which might be a very good thing, since I can't usually think myself into an illness based on heredity. When I talk with my own children about my past, it generally is limited to anecdotes rather than talks about ancestral heritage since it wouldn't be particularly accurate. I always gravitate towards Irish history because I was told that my birth father was born there and that coincides nicely with the history of my adoptive parents. While there is some comfort in feeling a part of that storied past, I can't reproduce an Irish brogue for the life of me – sure and begorrah!

One of the consequences of writing this piece is that I have decided to renew my efforts to discover my history. I have registered on two different online based sites for information about you and I presume they start with looking for a match. I have given them my birth name to see if someone else has initiated a search using that same name. I always find it a little disconcerting that I was given a birth name which was then changed by court order after my adoption a few days later. I didn't know until recently that this was a very common practice.

When I was much younger, I was given part of the documentation pertaining to my birth and adoption. There was a piece of stiff paper taped over some words of one of the documents in two different spots hiding what was obviously a name. I don't remember the details or timing but at some point, I rather daringly removed those pieces of paper to reveal a name typed in the spaces. I was under the clear impression that I was not supposed to know this information. I was not supposed to know my birth name. I do however remember wondering about that as a youngster. I would lie in my bed at night and consider the document that I had been shown with its hidden name and wonder when I would be able to discover it for myself. It has always been a subject of bewilderment as to why the authorities of that time would go to the trouble of taping over a name as though anyone would respect this cursory attempt to hide information. It is probably a very telling comment about that period of history and about the absolute respect and fear the populace had for authority in general. No wonder "the girls who went away" did so without protest, believing they were "doing the right thing." I remember the feeling of total disregard for this authority during the 1960's even though it was mixed with a surprising amount of fear for defying it. I always wondered what the consequences of removing the paper barrier might be. Some of this fear goes back to the times I was brought up in – the fifties. I imagine that this was even stronger for you. Authority was everything in the forties and fifties. You must have been very fearful as powerful figures like priests, parents and social workers advised you, or more probably told you, to give up your baby for adoption. Most young women of the day couldn't imagine defying this array of raw power.

Did you ever wonder about the incredible changes that occurred between the forties and sixties? How your generation completely submitted itself to the authority represented by teachers, politicians, parents, government, religion and even military. A generation later, we teenagers and university students defied all of that as we marched in the streets, sat in, burned effigies and refused all attempts to control us. How did you feel when you witnessed this complete about face? Did it produce anger or regret? Were you angry at these young people for their disregard of authority or did you look back in regret for your own generation's complete acquiescence to that same authority? What would you have done differently if you had grown up in the sixties? I still remember seeing bits of old black and white television broadcasts in which very serious U.S. senators blamed all the apparent moral turpitude and anti social behavior on the evils of rock and roll. In society's constant search for someone or something to blame, the blaming of popular music for anything connected to young people remains a consistent pastime to this day.

Fear and intimidation seemed to be a staple part of the diet and if my history serves correct, this had been the case for centuries, probably longer. It's not without some justification when we consider that the world was a pretty scary place prior to some huge technological advances that produced such things as electric light, automobiles, telephones and penicillin among many others. Interestingly, these inventions and discoveries all occurred during the late 1800's and into the 1900's. This would coincide with some of the prime years of your own parent's lives and would change the very nature of all that society accepted as normal. Up until then, everyone's life, like the planet itself, revolved around the sun that provided, not only warmth, but most importantly, light. Work, school and church took place during the daylight and at night the population huddled together indoors, safe from the dangers that lurked outside in the darkness with the cold black air and wild animals of all stripes.

What a revolution was started with all of these new inventions that defied everything that was held to be conventional wisdom since the beginning of time. Gradually, people were able to expand their universe with travel, light and medicine. The hold that parents had over their children, with all of the self evident dangers that swirled in the outside world, began to disappear. With the disappearance of the danger, fear and intimidation, people could start to stretch their wings of independence which would have created great consternation in parents, teachers, employers and religious figures that would have clung to their past ways in an attempt to control their minions. By the end of the Second World War this revolution would have been marching on several fronts as most homes had electric lights and radios, cars were fairly common, telephones connected ever increasing numbers and the war machine had produced substantial wealth, independence and confidence on this side of the ocean.

Society never moves from one era to the next in a smooth acceptable line of advance. But rather, it is pulled by its younger generations in fits and starts as the impatience of youth attempts to wrest control and create a new life in a multitude of ways, all at once. There is no grand plan or scheme, there is just varying amounts of pressure applied in sporadic thrusts as the older generation digs in its heels, resisting these same changes because they still hold a great fear of the unknown future. You must have felt this enormous pull on you from both sides when you found yourself pregnant and unmarried.

Those twin bastions of moral correctness, parents and the Church must have used everything in their power to make sure you felt all the blame, shame and guilt they thought you deserved. You would have been hidden from family, friends and neighbors and a story concocted as you were moved out of province to live with an aunt. It's a guess, of course, but I would imagine you were treated with complete disdain by an aunt who would sternly expect you to act the contrite slave girl to her imperious, stiff-backed morality. I'm also sure that no quarter was shown by the self appointed, god-like figures of the medical and social services communities either. What a place of loneliness and despair you must have found yourself in!

In some sort of back handed way, I suppose I have those same authorities, especially the Catholic church, to thank for my life as I'm also sure you would have been aware of an easier solution to your predicament. The fact that you didn't take the dark road to some back alley abortionist speaks more to your courage, to your character, your own moral compass than any set of man made rules from the imperial church and its leaders. Your brave decision to carry me to birth, in the face of enormous judgment from those around you, not only elicits my life long love for you but inspires my attempts at courage to follow your lead. Thank you for my life and that courage.

VIVA LA DIFFERENCE

All of my life, I have felt that I was different from other people. It probably started when I was very young, preschool, because of course, I was different than the other members of my family. I spent a lot of time over the years considering that same difference as it follows me to this day. It has always set me apart from other schoolmates, family, co-workers and friends. I don't know whether any of these people noticed it, but I did. They may have used words other than "different" to describe me; aloof, shy and arrogant come to mind as possibilities. As these kinds of feelings ferment over the years and decades, they become so ingrained and accepted that most of us (me included) don't even realize that they are there. We have built up a coping strategy around them that seems quite normal – it is who we think we are!

Feeling different leads, quite naturally, to a strong element of loneliness and once again we cope because we don't know what it is like to feel other than that. The interesting thing for me now is to realize that the essence of that "difference" that I felt as a child is actually my connection to you and my father. It is the combination of your genes that race through my veins and accounts for all of the hereditary characteristics that I have. Naturally, deep down, I simply must be different than the surroundings I was raised in and the adoptive family I grew up in, because in a cellular sense, I am more connected to my biological roots than my environmental ones. In my head, it all feels so logical.

The challenge, now that I am aware of the importance of "difference," is to distill out those different traits as they present clues to my heritage. These clues lead me to who you are and who my father is. They, in and of themselves, don't lead to names, addresses and personal histories but rather, these clues offer me a route to know some of the essence of my natural parents. To know who you were, what kind of persons you were, some of the deeper characteristics that would have been strong points in your lives. So now I get to look below the surface of my own life, at the things, feelings, perhaps even beliefs that made me different and try to discover those same traits that may have represented the guideposts in your life. If not environmental, then these traits must be the mixing of characteristics produced by the union between you and the young man who was my father.

I'm not sure if I have the skill to undertake this part of the journey but I now have the comfort of knowing that these differences represent the truth of who I am. You probably have no way of knowing how important this is to me. What always felt uncomfortable, what distanced me from the world is now my own essence, my core and truth.

I have mentioned intuition before. I feel as though I have some expanded ability in this area but I have no way of knowing whether that is true or not. My head and actually, that same intuition, tell me that all humans have huge wells of untapped intuition that most of us have yet to discover. Even discovered, most of us have neither the technical nor practical skills to make use of this intuitive ability. So, I'm not sure how this hooks up with the gene pool I rose from but why would I have this kind of heightened sensitivity to intuition unless perhaps I had some sort of genetic head start from you? An unprovable concept but nevertheless something to consider. It is difficult to decide whether some of my characteristics are the cause of my "differences" or the effect of those same differences.

I have always been very emotional in my reactions as opposed to my actions. I can remember bawling my eyes out as I watched Old Yeller being put down on the movie screen many, many years ago. I'm sure I repeated those feelings and tears when I saw it on the Disney show one Sunday night at home on television. Ditto for Bambi and many movies since then. I suspect this quick movement to tears is my natural response to seeing others in pain. I almost always feel tears well up in my eyes when I read about untimely deaths to children. When they interview grief-stricken parents, friends and family on the TV news, I find it impossible not to join these people in their emotions. Some friends of my son died in an avalanche a few years ago and of course the news of that tragedy and the ensuing funerals brought many tears, not surprisingly. But the thought of that event and those circumstances can and still do cause a lump in my throat and tears in my eyes several years later. The loss of children, or the losses experienced by children seem to be an especially strong trigger for an emotional response in me. I find it difficult to even contemplate the children of war around the world, the children abandoned to the streets in our own country and the children dying of drug overdoses, hunger and abuse in the so-called civilized nations on our planet. This entire line of thought tends to overwhelm me, first with grief and then I can feel a new emotion rising – anger.

I, once again, have no way of knowing or measuring my own emotions against the emotions of others to decide whether I am more or less sensitive to certain triggers but it would seem logical to me that my emotional response would in large part be a result of certain hereditary traits passed down from my natural parents. I accept those characteristics as a further connection to you and to my past – it gives me legitimacy. Isn't that an interesting word to finally introduce into this writing – legitimacy!

I hold a special loathing for the phrase "illegitimate child," a phrase created by some self serving, moralistic, judgmental, pinch-faced, strait laced matron of ignorance! Whew! I feel better now! For the edification of those same bastions of morality, it is not physically, spiritually or intellectually possible for any child to be illegitimate! Feel free to think of me as a bastard, if you wish but not illegitimate.

Earlier, I said that this heightened emotional response was a reaction. My tears came as a result of feeling grief, pain and loss and so I reacted in the only way I knew how – with tears. I can't remember a specific incident or time but during my very young and formative years, it became clear to me that this kind of response should be hidden. Somehow, it was not alright for a young boy to cry. Somehow, crying became a sign of weakness. Men don't cry! Another part of my life would now become a secret. It was alright for girls to cry but boys couldn't. It became very apparent that one of the worst accusations a young boy could hear was being like a girl! It is incredible how often, even in this day and age, that I have heard fathers, coaches and other male role models bark at their charges to stop crying or "acting like a little girl."

At this time in my life, I wonder why some emotions are considered feminine like fear, grief, sadness, emotional pain, even love and someone decided that they indicated weakness. Other emotions are considered a sign of strength, a sign of maleness like anger, hatred and aggression. So who decided which was which, who decided that we couldn't express all of the emotions? I know that every one of us feels all of those emotions but society, that same society that you must have wrestled with many years ago, has decreed that only some of us are allowed to feel, let alone express, specific emotions.

I swallowed that line of thinking for most of my life. Stoicism became my mantra. I couldn't prevent my feelings but I could hide them and hide them I did. To this day, most people including my immediate family, probably have no idea of my true feelings especially around grief and fear. When something on a television or movie screen produces tears, I am fairly adept at covering my eyes, clearing my throat and wiping my runny nose in secrecy. So this is very revealing for me to discover that I might have inherited those responses from you. My reaction to them would be a product of my environment, something created to protect myself from the outside world, but the emotion itself, I think, is inherited. Now I feel an even stronger link to you and my father as I can trace my emotional response to you and know that I am one step closer to my own truth. One step closer to connection with part of my history!

I wonder how many "normal" children take the chance to explore their past, their history, their roots, or their reason for being? Do they take it for granted? As an adoptee, I can take nothing for granted and so I am finally compelled to set out on this great adventure. I am now pulled to explore myself, my hopes, my desires, my regrets and failures along with my successes to discover who I am. I cannot assume that I know what I'm about because I can't hang my lineage on a hook and point to the past to explain the present or guide the future. So, I see this as a great benefit, setting aside assumptions allows me to create my life, to follow my natural instincts rather than the footsteps of others. Once again, I have reason to be grateful. It may sound contrived, but it is not so in my mind, I can be grateful to you, the mother who brought me into this world, the mother who gave me life. You allowed me this unique existence to become a man in my own right. There is a sense of freedom in having few ties that bind us to our past. We, all of us who are adoptees, don't so much need to make up our past as we have the opportunity to create our present and future free from the constraints of history. There is no one out there saying "Oh, you're just like your father!" – or mother, for that matter. We are just like ourselves, no preconceptions, no restrictions, free to create our future unfettered by either the successes or failures of our parents.

I always wondered why my factory-worker, adoptive father considered me a dreamer because I wanted more from life than I experienced as a child? He felt that being a dreamer was a bad thing. Perhaps as a reaction to that, I on the other hand, encourage my own children to dream. Dream as big as possible because possibility and reality come together at the end of that exercise. I truly believe that we are limited only by the size of the dreams we allow ourselves. What we focus on, we create. We make the choice to focus on lack, ill health, limitations and difficult circumstances or we can choose abundance, happiness and well being. I don't have any way of knowing whether these thoughts are hereditary or learned but if they are learned, then they took root in the attitudes of my adoptive family as I embraced my difference and rejected the influences around me in order to search for my own dreams.

There is some interesting information in a book called *"Freakonomics"* wherein the brilliant and highly decorated economist Steven Levitt cites genetics as the critical influence in young lives. He goes on to show through the results of various studies that adopted children tend to score lower marks in early schooling (that's me) but have an increased tendency towards higher education than those children reared by a single parent. Most of my higher education has been gleaned through my voracious lifelong reading habit. I have loved books, bookstores and libraries all of my life. One of my earliest memories is of the evening my adoptive mother and I rode the bus downtown to the public library. I was immediately transformed by the smell of books combined with old wood floors, paste wax and shelving. I even embraced the rule of silence and one of the proudest moments of my young life was when the stern librarian handed me a blue colored card that confirmed me as a junior member in good standing of the public library. I could now borrow a book, or maybe two or three and take them home with me to read. It opened an incredible world to me of high adventure, heroes and lands beyond my dreams at the time. The act of reading became second nature, became a necessity, a passion, became my own world to explore and enjoy and where dreaming was not just tolerated but encouraged. It seems to me that one of the reasons that reading has given me so much joy in life probably results from a blend of genetics and environment. Certainly, my adoptive mother was a reader and introduced me to the library and that world many years ago but the act of reading satisfies something deeper in my soul. It satisfies my need to explore, to experience adventure, to challenge beliefs of my own and others, to escape, to think and of course, to dream. It is not just the words on the page but the physical book itself that attracts me. I could then, and still can, spend countless hours in a bookstore or library in complete bliss. My only regret is the lack of time to read everything held there. My tastes run from best sellers by well known authors to cookbooks, biographies and holy crow, even an unlikely book entitled *"Freakonomics."* I don't think this passion can be explained simply by environmental factors in my young life, something else must be in play here.

Reading has been the most powerful influence in my life, without question. It has been too powerful to dismiss without wondering if the combination of genes that created me are not somehow responsible for this essential core of my existence. I can't prove this scientifically but reading has been such an overwhelming part of me that it dwarfs many other lines of influence. Reading satisfies my thirst for knowledge, it fuels my search for myself and my roots and provides safety and nourishment, a beacon of hope and sometimes, even an identity. Adoption has to figure into this story somehow and so I can't evade the powerful factors that played a role in my life as birth parents, adoption, adopted family and circumstances intertwined and perhaps offered books as my ancestry. It seems such a natural progression to go from reading to writing and without the combination of influences noted earlier, where would the twists and turns of fate have lead me?

One of the more curious facts about my life in recent years is how books find me. I'm not talking about the well known publications by authors I've been reading for years but rather, those books that have great influence on me and normally I would never intentionally search out. These are books that make me think, cause me to explore the inner workings of my mind, to consider who I am. Invariably, they come to my attention in odd sorts of ways. One day I was poking around the outdoor bunks of a bookstore sidewalk sale and while methodically reading the titles discovered one that caught my eye. Its title was

"Stages of the Soul: The Path of the Soulful Life." I skipped over it and kept looking for something else but frequently found my eyes returning to that slim volume until I finally picked it up and looked at it. I then discovered it was written by a Catholic priest named Father Paul Keenan and that almost sealed the deal. My first reaction was to put it back on the table and move on…quickly. This didn't sound like some quick lunch time read and in fact I knew that I wouldn't want any fellow diners seeing me with a title like that! Of course, my eye kept returning to it and so being unable to ignore it any longer I bought it, started reading it in my early morning quiet sessions, found it incredible, read it again, recommended it to friends and have since read some of Father Keenan's other works, as well. Brilliant book, brilliant find and I returned to that same bookstore on several occasions to buy more copies to give to friends but never did find any, books that is. People, who know me well, will be surprised that I would find wisdom and inspiration in the writings of a Catholic priest but good stuff is good stuff

regardless of its source not because of its source. Similar books have come to me over the years and I simply cannot explain how it happens. I could tell a similar story about another book entitled, "Shortcut to Spirituality: Mastering the Art of Inner Peace" by Bob Gottfried.

One day I was picking through the display tables lined up down the centre aisle of a large national book retailer. As usual, I had no particular goal in mind, I wasn't searching for anything specific, I was merely browsing in the true sense of the word. Looking at titles in the event something might look interesting and if it did, I would pick it up and glance at the dust jacket to learn what it was about. Most of the time, the topic didn't interest me and I moved on. On one of the last tables, a title caught my eye and I picked it up to read the back cover. The comments praising the book's contents and confirming what I thought the title referred to, held me enthrall. *"The Girls Who Went Away"* by Ann Fessler. I immediately knew what the title referred to, women like you, my birth mother, who were unwed and pregnant, who went to live in far away cities and give birth to their child. They left their baby behind and returned home with stories about caring for sick aunts. The book and its subject hit me like a ton of bricks and I marched straight to the cashier clutching this unexpected treasure.

It is a treasure! Ms. Fessler weaves her own story, as an adoptee in search of her birth mother, with the true life stories of young women who were, in most cases, forced to relinquish their babies. In all my years of life, I had never, until I read this book, even considered adoption from your perspective, from any birth mother's perspective. Some of the tales from the girls who went away are heart rending as they describe the pain of being forced to relinquish the babies who had been growing inside them for nine months. It changed my entire paradigm. The most amazing thing for me was to realize the number of similarities in issues that birth mothers share with their relinquished children. I had spent over fifty years of my life with a whole set of incorrect assumptions. Every case is different but the overwhelming evidence presented in Ms. Fessler's book indicates that the vast majority of girls gave up their babies under tremendous duress. That same majority have spent everyday of their lives wondering where their baby is and if he is safe. Once again, I have no scientific evidence only another assumption. I assume that the majority of adoptees like me, have spent their lives wondering about the whereabouts and safety and happiness of their birth parents. I discovered in this book that most of the girls felt abandoned by their families and came back from the loneliness of child birth feeling changed, different somehow, from their friends. They spent and still do, much time feeling ashamed and accepting the blame and scorn they received from parents, doctors, social workers, ministers and priests. They tried to hide their secret but the truth couldn't hide from their deepest thoughts. You, and they, carried this overwhelming guilt and a sense of longing. Longing to know the who's, and what's, and the where's and even the why's. Longing to be reassured, to know that they had done the right thing, longing to have their child say, "You did the right thing. I'm okay."

You did the right thing. I am okay.

ASSUMPTION

I have perhaps been a little too careful throughout my
life to not allow adoption to paint me as a victim. I
don't feel like I'm a victim of anything other than the
veil of secrecy created by those long ago bureaucrats
in social services and maintained to this day through
under funded government departments. There is a
significant body of research that would like to color
adoptees in the hues of victim-hood and maybe we
are, but maybe the real victims are the young women
like you. Young women who were forced to feel
unworthy, who were told that their child would be
better off without them, who were told that they
would forget all about this incident and go on with
their lives as though nothing had happened. Young
women who often entered child birth with no
information about what to expect physically and
certainly not emotionally. I read many accounts of
this process in Ms. Fessler's book, in which young

girls saw their babies, spent a few hours or even days connecting with, holding, feeding, touching their infants and then abruptly had their child taken from them. Many were forced or coerced into signing the release papers. Certainly, it seems that none of the young women I've read about, had anyone protecting their rights or offering any sort of alternative. I wonder about you, what kind of experience did you have? Did you see me after I was born, did you hold me, feed me, kiss me, say good bye to me?

Did you have options or alternatives?

Was anyone with you during childbirth?

Did anyone hold your hand, support you, inform you, comfort you?

Was child birth long, short, hard, easy?

What kind of after effects did you have?

What time of day or night did you give birth to me?

What was the weather like?

Did you stay in the hospital, did you see me the next day or anytime after?

When did you decide to put me up for adoption?

Did you ever regret that decision?

Did you ever try to discover my whereabouts?

Did you ever hear from my father again?

Did you ever marry, have other children – did you tell
them about me?

Where did you work, live, vacation, shop?

Do you cook, read, watch TV, walk, garden?

Do you enjoy the sun, the rain, hate the cold and
snow?

Are you drawn to the water or mountains or forest?

Do you gaze at the stars and clouds?

Do you wear glasses, get cold feet, dress well, drive a
car, like sports, go to the theatre?

Do you get sick, are you lonely, do you have
grandchildren, scrapbooks, pictures?

Are you still alive?

Do you celebrate Christmas, Easter, Thanksgiving?

When is your birthday?

Have you been to Europe, Africa, the Caribbean?

What are your major accomplishments,
disappointments?

What was your passion, your reason for being?

Are you politically left wing or right wing or do you prefer a drumstick? (sorry, sometimes I can't help it)

What is your favorite team, favorite flavor, color, memory?

Do you like to laugh?

What makes you cry?

Do you like jazz, rock, classical, big band?

Did you sing, dance, paddle a canoe, fix a flat tire?

Have you held a garage sale, painted a picture, collected collectibles, helped the poor, been the poor?

Did you go to church, the movies, the circus?

What's your perfume, soft drink, hard drink, lottery number?

Hair up, hair down, dress, pants, early, late, driver, passenger?

Do you speak French, Spanish, English or others?

When I reread the social services information recently, I noticed in their remarks about you that you liked to write. Wouldn't that be ironic but interesting? It's also interesting how we take information for granted. In a family, we often simply absorb it, especially little tidbits like someone's favorite food or color. I don't think most of us actually sit down with each other, brothers, sisters, mothers or fathers and ask a list of questions to try and discover the person we live with. Rather, we observe each other without thinking too much about it and probably assume a number of facts about one another. I can't do that with you mother. The only way to get to know each other would be to actually ask. If given the chance, the discovery process would probably lead to all sorts of similarities naturally, but more than a few differences I suspect as well. Another suspicion I harbor is that this business of "assuming" we know each other in "regular" family life can lead us astray pretty quickly.

I left home at the age of nineteen and in many ways, knowledge of my brother and two sisters became suspended at that point. I think, in many ways, their knowledge of me suspended at that point too. Consequently, we often think of each other using that old time frame as the benchmark for the persons we are now. We often assume that we know each other based on who we were many years, even decades ago. I wonder if that is true in other families because if so, then it could account for many of the misconceptions and incorrect conclusions that we draw about the beliefs, goals and even personal integrity and standards for one another. If my information is correct mother, then you came from a very large family. Do some of your brothers and sisters still treat you like the young woman who gave birth out of wedlock over six decades ago? Do they know the person you have become since then? What assumptions about who you are, do they incorrectly hold on to?

What assumptions am I making about you that are incorrect or perhaps correct? I often wonder when I look at my own children if I am looking at part of you. I think you would be very proud of them, as I am. One of the larger assumptions I am making is that the incident of my birth was much more than an "incident" to you. I assume that it was accompanied by much introspection, concern, decision making, angst and perhaps pain. I assume that you moved on from that to another life with occasional periods of wondering about me. I assume, for some reason, that you married and had a family. I have been reluctant throughout my life to be very aggressive in my search for you because of another assumption. I assumed, because I haven't had any inquiries from you or my father, that this part of your lives, my part, has been kept quiet, kept a secret. I assumed that if you have other children, my existence is unknown to them. I assume that is the choice you made. Because of these assumptions, I have not wanted to bring more pain or embarrassment to you. It would never be my intention to hurt you and so I have not hired private investigators, banged down the door of social services, nor instituted anything other than a passive registration of my birth name – just in case. At this moment, I have no idea what my reaction would be to some level of contact being requested by you, or my father or a half sister or brother. I know it sounds contrary when taken in context with this writing, but the whole idea of some sort of contact makes me very nervous. What about you? It's a little like winning the lottery – good news on the one hand but what would you actually do when confronted with the news? How would your life change? What are the possibilities? None of us are naive enough to assume that all of the possibilities are positive. In the case of birth reunions, I suspect the risks are very high. We both know that many, if not all, of our assumptions are probably incorrect. That's another assumption on my part, but how will we feel if those balloons get popped? I have revealed something of myself in these pages, but not everything. On your part, you might have to assume that what I have said is true in order to proceed. The risk – what if a key point I've made is wrong? Sometimes the risks are too high. Unlike the lottery, we have no defined reward. I'm sure, on your part, the lid might come off of a lifetime of pent up feelings and emotions. You might be exposed to the pain and guilt all over again. Would you be prepared to live with the same judgments that were inflicted upon you sixty years ago? Of course, one reward might be the sense of relief at having it out in the open. It's just a guess, but I wouldn't be too surprised if nobody but you and I, even cares about it.

This brings up yet another question for me, I wonder how the process of reunion and then the knowledge that comes with it, would affect my own children? Other than the obvious health information, what other ramifications could come of this? At the moment, they have family history information from their mother's side. On my side of the equation, if they have considered it yet, they must have some confusion. They were never able to meet my adoptive parents since they had died long before the birth of my children, so they are left with cousins, aunts and an uncle who passed away, that are part of my adoptive family. My kids know of my adoption, so they can observe some of the environmental traits but probably assume that their own genetic characteristics are largely from their maternal side. I will need to talk to them about this soon so that they are clear about what are known facts and what are not, about what is missing for them too. Sometimes of course, ignorance is bliss and I've talked about not having information about some predispositions and how it may allow me to live free from some assumptions regarding health. On the other hand, if I possess one of Shakespeare's "fatal flaws" then living in ignorance of it may indeed be fatal. Of course, all of our lives are eventually fatal anyway and since I have always been exceedingly healthy on a physical level, I will choose to pass that set of genetics on to my children and theirs, in as much as I have any control over it. There's nothing like a little deep-seated arrogance to perk up the genetic conversation.

In the book *"The Girls Who Went Away,"* the author interviewed over one hundred women, all of whom said that surrendering their child was the defining moment in their lives. I find this sad in two interconnected ways. If you, my birth mother, received the same advice given to these young women – that surrendering your baby would allow you to put this behind you – then you may have been sold a bill of goods too. If, like them, my birth was the defining moment in your life, did my birth prevent you from accomplishing something else in your life? It seems to me that making the birth and then the relinquishment of a child the defining moment in a woman's life, puts the lie to the stories and wisdom offered by all of those experts who assumed they knew what was best for you. In my mind, you would have every right to mourn, not only the loss of your child but clearly the loss of your life's purpose. The scope of this injustice is truly incredible as I realize that the number of relinquishing mothers count in the millions on a world wide basis. What advances and knowledge have been lost to your generation's version of political correctness, secrecy and shame? I suspect this generation's version of this failure may be even bigger as I observe the encouragement offered to middle class whites to adopt the children of radically different races, religions and cultures without a program or plan to assist these children as they grow older. I'm not talking about assistance in a financial sense but at some point, this lost generation is going to want to know who they really are and what their heritage is. Are there provisions in place to not only allow this process but are the processes going to help, hinder or hurt the parties involved? Have we learned anything from the past? How can we, when we keep it blanketed in secrecy and political correctness? Genetics trump environment, we are told by numerous studies. How does this fact play a role in the adoption procedures of today? The cynic in me gets concerned when I see the Hollywood set embracing intercultural adoption and parading their humanitarian deeds along with their new child in the pages of celebrity magazines and television interview shows. Are they creating some kind of private hell for these children who may not be ready for the publicity fishbowl of the "stars?" Is it wise to take young children from abject poverty, the horrors of war, death and disease and thrust them overnight into the circus of nannies, wealth and media – something they have never witnessed, let alone experienced. Should we expect some repercussions and if so, what kind of reaction, help and support is planned and available? The act of adoption is an exercise in pure love, courage and faith with many pitfalls along the way. Have the various social agencies involved created a program of assistance that will parallel the needs and concerns of both the children and adopting parents as they grow through the various stages of their lives? Is there a responsibility to do this? Don't we have enough evidence and research available to design a system of support? When the adoption papers are signed, the process of adoption is just beginning, not concluding. I am not against intercultural adoption, I am just against entering into this life long contract without some knowledge of what the future holds for all parties including the adoptee, the relinquishing mother and perhaps father. There are enough adoptees and relinquishing mothers around North America, we number in the millions, so that we may be able to offer some assistance in creating a sustaining program of help based on our own experience and expertise.

It occurs to me that if we gathered together in conference, a group of psychiatrists, psychologists, medical practitioners, social workers and other experts who were themselves adoptees and relinquishing parents, they might come up with some worthwhile advice for today's participants. No mere academic based degree substitutes for reality. They might also shed some light for those of us already caught in this web of secrecy, fear and confusion. This is not just a North American issue because so many of the children involved come from the so called third world – this is a global issue affecting millions and leadership on the level of the United Nations seems to be called for. Society has been reactive, at best, to the issues surrounding adoption. It is well past time to become proactive not just to avoid potential problems but to fulfill the promise of a better world for adoptees and to provide comfort and respect to the relinquishing mothers who have been left to twist and wonder and cry in their own private hell.

I am very lucky in many ways. Being white, Christian, born and raised in North America, growing up in a middle class family, having good schools, access to jobs, television, books and a certain societal tolerance for various youthful indiscretions, has given me many advantages that some of today's adoptees might not be able to hope for. I didn't spend any time in an orphanage and would have a hard time pointing to an incident in my immediate family that would differentiate me from my two natural-born siblings in any way, even to this day. I didn't experience any kind of prejudice or bullying based on having parents of a different race or religion. I was made aware of my adoption before my teen years and I don't recall the telling as particularly traumatic. I had my share of traumatic incidents in my youth but can't honestly point to adoption as playing any particular role in them. I assume (there's that word again) that most people experienced some drama and trauma in their teen aged lives, mostly self inflicted, but part of a normal growing and learning process. I can recall a few out of place comments by some adults as I was referred to as a step-brother in one case and as "not a real Bannon" in another. The sources of these and a few other remarks were not particularly credible at the time and the attitudes presented by my brother and sisters have always held much more sway over me than some ill considered remarks by people who didn't know our relationship. If I had to go out and choose siblings, I could not have made a more fortunate choice than the loving, loyal and absolutely rock-solid three that I am lucky enough to call my brother and sisters. I don't make these comments lightly and that old saw about being able to choose your friends but not your family doesn't apply for me. I truly had the best of both worlds, a family that chose me, loved me, defended me and supported me – they still do.

My gratitude runs in two directions. To the family I was adopted into and to you, my birth mother for allowing that possibility to exist. I look around at other "natural families" and often see dislike, pain, resentment, jealousy, lack of communication and depth as real and imagined hurts have created rifts over the years. Perhaps it is the lack of a blood connection that has created a life long friendship for us. Like many things, it is impossible to determine if the adoption of me or my sister into this family has created some sort of mutual respect or tolerance but it seems to exist none the less.

FATHER

As a male, I have a natural curiosity about my father. The information provided by the children's aid society is flattering as well as sketchy. Their version of events has him wanting to marry you and when that didn't work out, he apparently supported you financially through pregnancy. It would be interesting to learn your memories as they relate to these facts. It would be more interesting to hear you discuss who he was and what he was like. It would be interesting to discover what similarities we share. In the readings and conversations about adoption, the father is generally given rather short shrift. It seems that the stereotypical unwed father flees the scene at his first opportunity. Is this always the case? Of course, he didn't have to bear the responsibility for carrying a child for nine months like you did. Nor did he make the lifelong connection that follows. Does it also follow that just because the young father-to-be didn't have the physical burden of pregnancy that he didn't perhaps bear some emotional and psychological baggage instead? We assume that most unattached young men treat this sort of thing like a hit and run accident. As soon as the deed, or is that seed, has been done, they flee into the night unexposed, unencumbered and unburdened. In your day mother, and for many decades prior and since, the male partner in the creative process seemed to escape scot-free. This is certainly the picture painted by every source I have consulted. I do wonder though if he remains free of guilt, free of association with you or me. Does he assume, like most people of that time, that the fault and the responsibility of becoming pregnant rested with you? We have almost no information, studies or facts about unwed fathers other than anecdotal evidence provided by their partners in the unwanted pregnancy. We are left, once again, to assume. As a reasonably typical male, I may be accused of protecting the guilty, but I wonder if it is wise to assume that there is no caring or sense of responsibility just because it hasn't been presented in evidence by unwed fathers. As a father, I can't imagine that these young men could enter into a marriage later in their lives, have children and not think about the child they had already fathered. I am left to wonder what ramifications that thought process might have. It seems reasonable that some degree of guilt and shame must have ridden on their shoulders. Years of suppressing and hiding those emotions, acknowledged or not, must lead to some degree of anger and disappointment turned inward, one could assume. This may give unwed mothers some degree of satisfaction, to know that the burden you have carried all these years was in some way a shared one after all.

The butt of the locker room joke is the guy who answers a knock on the door and is greeted by a stranger saying, "Hi Dad." In that same locker room, where testosterone and male ego mix to produce many tales of exploits both real and imagined, some indiscretions are still closely guarded. Not very many men are going to voluntarily disclose in an open forum that they fathered an "illegitimate" child because their listeners rapidly make the leap from unwed fatherhood to abandonment of both mother and child. I've never been in a locker room atmosphere where admitting that fact carries any humor or pride. It might take a bottle of scotch to pry information such as this from most men but it would be followed with much remorse the next morning. Remorse for the admitting more that the consumption in most cases. Aside from all the male bluster, most of their peers would look upon abandonment with a dim view unless attempts had been made to "do the right thing." Consequently, and pun intended, mum's the word. All of this assumes that the father is even aware that he has created a life. I wonder how many wander through life not knowing that there are children following in their wake, unknown to each other and I wonder, if confronted, whether the majority of men would deny the possibility? Is it right, fair or even reasonable to make these assumptions? I don't feel any particular right to presume what a man should or shouldn't do if confronted with a child produced decades earlier in a relationship long since ended. I can only say that in my own case, if I had the opportunity to meet my birth father, I would only do so because of my own interest in him, not because I wanted anything other than knowledge in return.

Mother, this is the case for both of you – I only seek knowledge. Whatever fears you may harbor about my intentions, it is crystal clear to me that information about my history is the only purpose that I have. I have wrestled with this whole thing throughout my life and I can't go beyond the first step – one step at a time with mutual consent required to even consider a next one. Do you share my curiosity about physical characteristics, likes, dislikes, habits and traits?

I don't know if this will spell relief or disappointment but when I think of my parents, I think of my adoptive parents. They are the people who raised me, guided me, set an example, tolerated my many foibles, sheltered and clothed me. Both have long since passed on, so this exercise that I have entered into, won't bring hurt to them. If they were still alive, I have a suspicion that they might both support this writing – at least, I find comfort in that assumption. It may sound like too fine a distinction to some, but for me, parents are different than mother and father. That title, in my mind, is reserved for you. It may not be one you relish or accept, especially from me, but there it is for all who read this, to see.

REUNION

I'm sure most would agree that reunions must create a very highly charged atmosphere as two intimate strangers attempt to rise above their own feelings to find common ground. Emotions, questions, answers buried in anger, shame and secrecy, doubts, assumptions, hopes and expectations all swirl in a cauldron heated by fear. On your part, I suspect there would be fear of more blame from the exposure; how will this affect your current relationships with a spouse or children, especially if they were unaware of me? This matches up with my fears, the adoptee who worries about being rejected again as the subject of a lifetime of ills. I know that I represent a threat to you and probably even more so to any subsequent children you might have had. They may see me as a threat for your affections and attentions. A part of your life left behind long ago can't resurface without repercussions that might threaten the tranquility of the life you have built today. What is interesting to me is the realization that I share those same fears and threats. I have been able to make up my life without regard to the truth, because I don't know what the truth is. That insight provides some interesting avenues for self discovery. Consequently, I threaten to shatter the assumptions and illusions that I have used as guides throughout my existence. It has repercussions for my own family who can't possibly understand why I feel an emptiness and a need to fill it. They would feel at risk of another family member entering their lives and how would that affect their own place? How would they be expected to treat her, a potential subject of the limited affections that I dispense already? My children might be too young and otherwise engaged to sense a certain rejection of them, as well. I wonder if this lack of history on their father's side already has some effect or if it will later, as they have children of their own?

The risks and rewards of this reunion dance are tenuous at best. Those around us, our families, feel subject to many of the risks and probably can't see any reward. The rewards for us can only come after more pain, pain held in check until now, pain buried beneath the mists of time, pain carried in a deep place no one but we, can penetrate. To resurrect that pain, long felt but left unacknowledged, seems almost reckless and would be sure to bring into question our very sanity as it tested our need for completion.

Should you ever have the opportunity to actually read this, there may be some value in knowing what some of the questions are in advance. Knowing what I am looking for in my quest for a past, helps me to focus my thoughts and neutralizes some of the emotional charge surrounding memories you probably thought best forgotten. Let's start with who you are:

Where were you born?
Who were your parents?
Where did they come from?

What did they do?

How old were they when you were born?

When did they die?

Tell me about your brothers and sisters.

Which was your favorite and why?

Do they have families?

Where do they live?

What do they do?

Where did you go to school? For how long?

What did you like about school? Hate?

Did you have other interests, hobbies, sports, friends?

What was life like at your childhood home?

What were your plans, dreams, aspirations?

Did you fulfill them?

Did you finish high school and go on to any other education?

What illnesses, broken bones and other ailments did you have?

What was your sense of childhood? Was it happy, sad?

How did you meet my father? Where? When? How old were you? How old was he?

Where did you live? Big house, small house?

What city, street?

Did you share your bed with siblings?

Did you have favorite movie stars? Books? Radio programs?

What were your favorite foods? Flavor of ice cream?

Did you have favorite musicians?

How have your tastes changed over the years?

Did you work?

What was your first job? Where? What did you do?

What can you tell me about my father?

What was his name?

What was your relationship like?

What did he do – work-wise?

Was he in the war?

Did you know his parents?

Did he have brothers and sisters?

What kind of person was he?

How did he treat you? Before? After?

Can I assume pregnancy was a mistake?

How pregnant were you when you found out?

What was your reaction?

What was the reaction of your parents? Family?
Friends?

What was my father's reaction?

What decisions did you then have to make?

What plans did you put in place?

Were you in control or was someone else?

Could you have married? Why didn't you?

What were your choices?

Have you second guessed yourself since?

If you could go back to that time – what would you
change?

When you were pregnant with me, did you work?

Where did you live?

What was it like?

What was my birth like for you?

Did you see me after?

What was it like to sign the papers releasing me?

What did you feel then?

After that experience, what did you do?

Where did you live and work then?

Did you get married?

Did you have more children? How many?

If so, what are they like?

What are their names? Where are they?

Do they have families?

Would you want me back in your life?

How would I fit?

Do you suppose we would recognize each other?

What can I do to ease your mind?

How can I bring peace to your life?

The exercise of writing this letter, this book, has had a very cathartic effect for me. One of my major purposes has been to provide some sort of similar effect for you. I have wanted to let you know that although you may have suffered in ways untold, your actions and decisions surrounding my birth and relinquishment have created a well of gratitude in my heart. I have no access to any parallel universe, so I can't see what differences would have occurred if you had made any decisions differently. Except, of course, the big one. Had you not become pregnant, I wouldn't be here today! That's pretty big to me. I suspect that it is pretty big to you too, only in a much different way.

You will have suffered the judgments of society and those around you or you may have suffered the self judgment in silence but more likely both. You suffer no judgment from me. I wonder if a statistic I read recently is true. If so, then a very large number of people in North America are affected by this event when you consider the adoptees, the relinquishing parents, the adoptive parents, siblings, spouses and offspring. We number in the millions as a group with little or no voice or connection. I can't decide if that increases or decreases the feelings of loneliness – how about you? It certainly increases the feelings of frustration when I consider the indifference we suffer from the various "child rights" proponents in government. Access to information has opened up tremendously in some jurisdictions but there is still great resistance to allowing millions of previous-generation mothers and adoptees to obtain even rudimentary information about their roots or the children they bore. The frustration heightens as we realize that today's bureaucrats and experts approve open adoptions and all sorts of information and even physical exchange and access and proclaim it to be beneficial. In the meantime, they lock the doors proclaiming the very same benefits of secrecy to millions of others. The rich and famous jet set from Rodeo Drive to Africa, scoop up an infant, return to the media spotlight and the spin of their publicists while an older generation begs for scraps of medical information – no names released, of course. Today's unwed, teenaged mother and her supportive parents, participate in the lives and decision making of their relinquished offspring in concert with its adopting parents under the approving eye of an "open society" while doors to information are firmly, and none too politely, slammed in the faces of a previous generation. Do you also feel as though we are milling about in this field of isolation, closed off, ignored and looked upon as somewhat embarrassing, while most of society just sort of hopes that we will go away. The march of time will ensure that this eventually happens but that doesn't excuse the failure of the responsible institutions of church and state for creating lost generations who suffer in secrecy, if not silence.

Some of that anger is resurfacing again but it is clearly directed at the circumstances beyond our control. It is directed at the unwillingness of authorities who possess information who feel that it threatens their power base to release that same information. Perhaps they feel that the release of information may make their own lives purposeless. I seem to be approaching the writing of a sequel with this line of thinking. It would have something to do with approaching sensitive and controversial issues with common sense – a foreign concept to some, it seems.

Those thoughts are for another time and place and I return to my original purpose in writing this missive – you, my birth mother. Regardless of what happened to either of us following my birth, neither we, nor anyone else, can deny that you are a mother and I am your son. We are linked together through birth, life, death and perhaps beyond. This link cannot be expunged by legal documents, ignorance, time, circumstances, secrecy, denial or wishing it were so.

We can face it, ignore it, embrace it, regret it, reject it, blame it, love it, hate it, hide it, parade it or fear it but we cannot change it. We are linked through eternity, a link forged in the fires of separateness and longing, a link left to be healed in this life or the next, a link made stronger for the breaking. The lives and history of my birth mother and birth father remain beyond my grasp, still elusive and undiscovered. Like shells on the beach, clues are strewn throughout my life to show me the path that connects to who I am. I'm not sure if hints that tease me with the truth are enough but they suffice at this moment in time. I listen to others wax poetic about their storied past, as their ancestors realized dreams and they connect with the generations who marched through history to wash up on the shores of today. It evokes some envy and awe and wonder as I observe their pride in the telling of their family story. A certain melancholy floats on the breeze but the mystery remains intriguing and I'm tempted to let my imagination have free rein. Pulled back by my need to manage my hopes so as not to be disappointed, a balance is struck between the absence of reality and the presence of dreams. Reality and dreams reside within me and each is interdependent, relying on itself and the other to provide truth, purpose, clarity, history and future. I return to the waves on that long ago beach and feel the connection between earth, water and stars and know that my universe has unfolded in all of its glory, just exactly the way it needed to.

I am surrounded by clues to my identity. Unlikely sources of information most often ignored but persistent in their constant assurance, if only I choose to accept their presence. I search through these pages for my secret mother, often wondering about my purpose and intent.

If not reunion, then union confirmed.
I am okay - and thank you - for my life.

MICHAEL JOSEPH RIOUX

a few post writing thoughts

Writing a book, even a small one like this, is a very interesting experience. It is truly wonderful to read the compliments and excitement of family and friends who take the time to read and send a letter or email. I think that inside every reader is a frustrated writer and we either use the frustration to motivate our writing or we suffer with the frustration of not having done it. In any case, when you write about yourself, it becomes a cathartic event with feelings bubbling up and taking effect in all sorts of unimagined ways.

The day I had the phone call from the social worker referred to at the very beginning of this book, I literally felt weak at the knees and as I attempted to explain what had just taken place to a co worker, found myself needing to take several deep breaths in order to calm down.. There was a strong "butterflies in the stomach" clamminess that crept over my body and a palpable shaking of my insides going on. The contact was unexpected but the news that my father actually existed and that someone had just talked to him about me, was unbelievable. I can't imagine that anyone who is not adopted could possibly relate to this swirling mixture of fear, joy, trepidation and happiness.

Since sending the book to him, I have had no further contact with anyone including him and that was what my intellect expected after the social worker told me that he didn't want to meet but wished me a good life. I had included a letter with the book that I sent to the social services department to forward to my father and have since wondered if he received the book or the letter. I still sit in limbo both for wondering if he received them and wondering, if in fact he did, what was his reaction. In my heart I am still a little disappointed because I imagine that he may have read some of my innermost thoughts and I still hope for some sort of contact. My heart would like the connection while my mind still understands why he may not be able to.

The Christmas following the sending of the

book to my father, we decided to start a new tradition in our family. At dinner, we set an extra place and took turns in declaring who might be the unexpected guest or who we might like to have joined us. I named my birth father, not by name but by title, since that is all I have. I can't explain my lack of initiative regarding the search for either parent. I suspect that finding my birth mother would not be particularly difficult since I know my last name, etc. My ego perks up a bit when I realize that no one has apparently searched for me either. I know that there is a hurt little boy still lurking inside but I have chosen to get on with life rather than dwell on what might have been.

I have experienced the questioning provided by many people, including adoptees, wondering why I haven't immediately gone into overdrive to locate both of my parents (assuming my mother is still alive) and force some sort of meeting. As much as I would like to give them an answer, I would also like to discover an answer for myself, but have been unsuccessful at doing so. I don't think that I am afraid of what I might find because I have already found more than I expected. If anything, I would be afraid to discover that I was completely unwanted and still might be. That is not meant to be maudlin but I really have no need to create some sort of hate, blame, poor-me-victim, in this thing. I have spent an inordinate amount of time producing this book and must admit that I bounce back and forth between releasing it and burying it, a lot like my attitude toward finding my parents. This is one of the areas in my life in which I have a lot of trouble making a decision, yet I continue to review and edit and prepare for some sort of release. Even the method of release is a sort of confused future event at this writing. I don't know if this ambivalence is common to others in the adoption cycle but I do know from research, that rarely does the reconnection have the ending that both parties had hoped for.

I would like to offer my apologies for any inaccuracies or discrepancies that have caused hurt to family members and public readers alike. I have tried to be objective and sensitive but the paradigm, like the incorrectness, is mine. I offer my eternal gratitude to those people who have influenced my life and this writing in ways that you will never be able to comprehend. I thank you for your support, encouragement, tolerance, love and suggestions. If this offering can help one person in the adoption cycle reach a level of understanding and peace, then it will have been a success.

Robert J. Bannon
bannon.bob@gmail.com
Calgary, Canada

If you enjoyed reading MY SECRET MOTHER, I would appreciate it if you would go to Amazon and post a comment on the book's or author's page. Thank You

OTHER BOOKS BY ROBERT J. BANNON

THE WEST COAST TRAIL: One Step at a Time

THE ONE HOUR AUTHOR: non-fiction book writing for busy people

ALL BOOKS ARE AVAILABLE ON BOTH AMAZON AND KINDLE AND ALSO FOR OTHER ELECTRONIC DEVICES.

CONTACT:

www.RobertjBannon.com

http://bookmentor.blogspot.com/
for early stage authors

http://mindgas-bobb.blogspot.com/
a blog of random thoughts and ideas

BookBob on Twitter

BIBLIOGRAPHY:

THE GIRLS WHO WENT AWAY
The hidden history of women who
surrendered children for adoption in the
decades before Roe vs. Wade

by Ann Fessler

ISBN 9781594200946

FREAKONOMICS
A rogue economist explores the hidden side
of everything

By Steven D. Levitt and Stephen J. Dubner

ISBN 9780061234002

MY SECRET MOTHER:

An adoptee speaks to the girls who went away

MY SECRET MOTHER:

An adoptee speaks to the girls who went away

MY SECRET MOTHER:

An adoptee speaks to the girls who went away

MY SECRET MOTHER:

An adoptee speaks to the girls who went away

MY SECRET MOTHER:

An adoptee speaks to the girls who went away

MY SECRET MOTHER:

An adoptee speaks to the girls who went away

18183404R00081

Made in the USA
San Bernardino, CA
04 January 2015